THE MINISTRY (& MYTH) OF THE FIRST LADY

A Handbook For Leading Ladies in Ministry

Apostle Clifford E. Turner, Ph. D.

Bloomington, IN   Milton Keynes, UK

Cedar Life Publishing
Olympia Fields, IL
"Preserving the Life Within"

AuthorHouse™
1663 Liberty Drive, Suite 200
Bloomington, IN 47403
www.authorhouse.com
Phone: 1-800-839-8640

AuthorHouse™ UK Ltd.
500 Avebury Boulevard
Central Milton Keynes, MK9 2BE
www.authorhouse.co.uk
Phone: 08001974150

First published by AuthorHouse 4/17/2006

ISBN: 1-4259-2587-1 (e)
ISBN: 1-4259-2586-3 (sc)

Library of Congress Control Number: 2006902875

Unless otherwise noted, all Scripture quotations are from the
King James Version of the Bible.

Printed in the United States of America
Bloomington, Indiana

This book is printed on acid-free paper.

This book is dedicated to all of the powerful, anointed, and chosen leading ladies of this day. As you continue to press on towards the mark of this high calling, may you be perfect and entire, wanting nothing.

TABLE OF CONTENTS

FOREWORD

The first lady has been such a vital, yet obscure, function in the church, often generating much debate regarding the validity of her role. Many church leaders neglect the position of first lady, considering it unbiblical and non-essential. Others overemphasize and abuse the function and authority of the pastor's wife, and help to breed the stereotype of the big-hat-wearing, non-stop-shopping, big-jewelry-wearing, looking-good- but-having-no-real-substance woman behind the man of God.

This book, without debating the validity or biblical correctness of the role, addresses the characteristics that are necessary for every first lady, pastor, or other woman of God in ministry. All too often we, in the Kingdom of God, have failed to be trained and failed to receive wisdom regarding our various roles, responsibilities, and expectations (both God's and men's). The Bible says*, "My people perish for a lack of knowledge"* – not for lack of prayer, lack of conferences, lack of fasting, or lack of prophetic words – **lack of knowledge!** The Bible further states that *"In all of our getting, get understanding."* In a society that now often lacks many of the foundational essentials that were taught in the home, there is an unprecedented need to address issues that at one time may have been thought to be "common."

My husband, Dr. Clifford E. Turner, has written this book in his never-ending quest to help women in ministry who have been placed in areas of great authority and responsibility. This book was written from the notes of a first lady's class, taught by my husband for women who believed that God was calling them into ministry. I was a student of the class (taught more than twelve years ago), although not his wife at the time. (That's another book!) I can attest to the honesty, validity, and need for many of these issues to be addressed. Even for those of us who know many of the requirements, *The Ministry (& Myth) of the First Lady*, helps us to reexamine ourselves, to "see if we be in the faith," and to have our "call" confirmed.

In many of the references in this book, my husband refers to his first wife, and my former first lady, Co-pastor Denise M. Turner, to whom he was married for over twenty years before she went home to be with the Lord. This book is dedicated to her memory, because she truly exhibited the love, maturity, generosity, wisdom, patience, attitude, sense of family, and commitment to her call of being "the first lady." She was key in the building of Liberty Temple Full Gospel Church (which began with two members). Since its inception, it has expanded to more than fifteen locations nationwide (as of this printing), sixteen nations outside the United States, and a network of thousands of individuals, businesses, and ministries.

My prayer is that every first lady, woman in ministry, or woman of God seeking to be blameless before our Father, will read this book. The insight and wisdom it contains, when read with an open heart, will help every woman who reads it to ascend to a higher level in faith, love, and character. I trust that you, too, will allow *The Ministry (& Myth) of the First Lady* to aid you in your march towards perfection.

Elect Lady Darlyn C. Turner

INTRODUCTION

God has entrusted women with power, influence, and mighty purpose. Personally, a female apostle mentored me and I have several women pastors in my fellowship. I thank God that they have been godly examples of strength, grace, and humility. However, over the course of my thirty years in ministry, there has seemingly been an uprising of independent and unsubmitted women in ministry who are leading masses of women down the path of pride and arrogance, under the disguise of "freedom."

Please do not get me wrong. There are many wonderful, anointed, submitted, and powerful women of God. However, there are an alarmingly increasing number of women successful in ministry who have gained popularity and prestige, but who are poor examples of loving, caring, and committed virtuous women. God is still calling for the Naomis of this age to mentor the Ruths. The wisdom principles of life are still the same as they were more than 2,000 years ago. A soft answer still turns away wrath, and it is still unwise to *"answer a fool, lest you become like him."*

Every first lady, pastor, and Christian must understand that wisdom is the principal component of being successful in life, successful in God, and successful in ministry. The Bible says wisdom is the **principal** thing. This means that wisdom is that which is first in priority, preeminent, and most necessary. Without wisdom, ladies, you, your ministry, your marriage, and your family will die a sure and sudden death. I am not speaking negatively, but the Bible makes it clear that without "her" (wisdom), destruction, death, poverty, and shame are inevitable.

First ladies must be women of wisdom. They must be women who not only seek knowledge, but also learn how to apply it. Otherwise, they will be "ever learning" but never coming into the knowledge of the truth. Or, to put it another way, you can know Scriptures, have revelation, know how to preach, prophesy, and be gifted, but if you do not know how to walk in love and patience when it is required in everyday situations, you only have knowledge – and not wisdom.

Women in ministry must be examples of wisdom as wives and mothers, in business and in ministry. It will be their wisdom and discretion that will preserve them and bring them to a place of honor, glory, prosperity, and purpose. Too many first ladies I have seen are just smart, but not wise. A smart woman knows how to save her money, but a wise woman knows how to sow. A smart woman looks out for herself, but a wise woman prefers others over herself. A smart woman stands up for her rights, but a wise woman knows righteousness must transcend rights.

I believe you are — because you are reading this book — a wise woman seeking wisdom, knowledge, correction, and truth. I am in agreement with you that you will come into the fullness of Christ and you will walk out the good and perfect will that God has for you, your family, and your ministry.

Apostle Clifford E. Turner, Ph.D.

CHAPTER ONE

THE FIRST LADY - DEFINED

"Even so must their wives be grave, not slanderers, sober, faithful in all things."

I Timothy 3:11

In I Timothy 3, Apostle Paul set forth the requirements of the church leaders, particularly the men, admonishing them to be: blameless... sober...of good behavior...apt to teach...not double-tongued...not greedy of filthy lucre, etc. In that chapter as well as in other books and chapters of the Bible, the requirements for female leaders and first ladies are also described (for example, see I Timothy 3 and I Peter 3).

However, the core premise of being a first lady is very simple and can be summed up as this: First ladies should be "first" in being a "lady."

I believe that the "art" of being a lady has been somewhat lost in today's society. In the quest for freedom, equality, and equal rights, even the church has begun to divert from some of the "old landmarks" that should not be removed. The very term "first lady" clearly defines the essence of what the individual who holds its title should reflect.

Let's look further into the makeup of the term "first lady," beginning with the definition of "first."

"First" is defined as:

- Coming before or above all others in time, order, rank, or importance.
- Occurring or acting before all others in time; earliest.
- Ranking above all others in importance or quality; foremost.

"Lady" is defined as:

- A well-mannered and considerate woman with high standards of proper behavior.
- A woman regarded as proper and virtuous.
- A woman who is the head of a household.

-A woman, especially when spoken of or to in a polite way.

-A woman of refinement.

So, then, what is a first lady?

FIRST LADY

A woman who is head of a household, considered to be foremost in her profession, whose character and behavior ranks above others, and whose positive actions precede others.

"First lady" has nothing to do with lifting yourself up in pride or haughtiness, or being a big "I" surrounded by little "yous"; but it has everything to do with being first in honor, courage, and responsibility, and being a godly example.

CHAPTER TWO

THE CALL

"Many are called, but few are chosen..."

Matthew 22:14

The office of a first lady is just that – an office. It is a place of authority, a position, and a call. The call refers to being invited and summoned. Every woman who stands beside her husband in ministry, whether she can sing or not, play the piano or not, prophesy or not, has been invited and summoned by God to a position of authority and responsibility that requires wisdom, sacrifice, commitment, and understanding.

Accept and Understand the Call

You must first consciously and deliberately accept and understand that you have been called. If you do not recognize the call, you are certainly not fulfilling the commission. You must "count up the costs" of this call and make a decision to give up your own life so that the life that Christ has for you may be revealed.

> *First ladies must not only receive mentoring, but know also that there is a need for training.*

There are many women in ministry who have accepted the call to serve God – so they think. However, many have never really accepted the *fullness* of the call. How do you know? You know because the call to anyplace in ministry is accepting the call to die! If you refuse to die to your old mindset, personal preferences, likes, dislikes, doing things your own way, responding negatively to people, and a questionable belief system, you really have not accepted the call.

Every disciple whom Jesus called had to walk away from something. Every one of them had to leave that which was familiar – family, traditions, and places – to wholly and completely dedicate themselves to the call.

Some women in ministry pride themselves by saying, "Well, this is just the way I am." What they are really saying is, "I have not developed social skills or the ability to interact with others." To those women, God would say, "You have not died yet."

Then, some women have a certain style of dress that is not appropriate for women in ministry, while others fear the loss of their freedom if they come to a certain place of submission. All of these women do not recognize that the price of their call requires a denial of some of their personal preferences, which is, once again, the need to die to self.

Too many saints have just opted to "follow Christ," but failed to "take up their cross." Jesus said, ***"Take up your cross and follow me"*** (Matthew 16:24). In other words, you cannot just tiptoe through the tulips, honey. The cross represents suffering, denial, and the dying of your flesh. Unless you first accept the call to die to yourself, you really cannot truly follow Christ.

A favorite hymnal that we sang in the Baptist church puts it like this: *"Must Jesus bear the cross alone and all the world go free? No, there's a cross for everyone and there's a cross for me."*

Remember, the call to something is always a call from something!

Count Up the Costs

Secondly, after you have accepted the call, count up the costs and resign yourself to the death of self (the death of your ways, your ideals, and your thoughts – replacing them with God's ways, God's ideals, and God's thoughts). You need to get some understanding and wisdom in how to fulfill this tremendous call so that you may be not only the called, but also the chosen.

> *Accept the call, count the costs, and resign yourself to the death of self.*

I have been in ministry for almost thirty years, and I sadly report that too many first ladies and women in ministry have pursued things – getting speaking engagements, getting jewelry, St. John suits, houses, and lands, but have forgotten that *"In all of your getting, get understanding!"*

As a first lady, or woman in ministry, you must understand that most important is being a woman of prayer. Then you can operate in power and fulfill God's purpose for your call. It is also important for you to know that your purpose and plan may be drastically different from that of your counterparts. However, it is through your

> *It is through your relationship with God that your purpose and call will truly be revealed.*

4

relationship with God, through prayer, and through your submission to the God-ordained authorities in your life that your purpose and call will truly be revealed.

There are key components of your call to ministry that must be understood. Esther is the best example of a "first lady." She was called for a specific purpose, she was a woman of prayer, and she submitted to the spiritual authority in her life (Mordecai). Therefore, she was able to appropriate God's grace and power. In a nutshell, this is exactly how the kingdom works, whether male or female, first lady, prophet, or apostle. God has placed a call on your life before the foundations of the world. Then, He puts you in the right family (it was the right one, whether you believe it or not), and assigns you to a spiritual authority figure. As you (like Esther) grow in grace, character, and obedience to both God **and** man, you will be led to your ultimate purpose.

Esther (like most of you) did not ask for this call; she was summoned. Esther was then groomed and prepared for her call. This is a very critical point that has generally been missed in the Kingdom of God. Her appointment as queen was just the beginning of her responsibilities and ultimate purpose for her position. She was not placed in the coveted position of queen for her own enjoyment and comfort.

Ladies, I have to stop right here for a moment. I need to be your spiritual Mordecai today and bring some things to your remembrance:

You must stay focused on why you are where God called you. You are not "in the palace" so you can look good, drive good, and live large. Therefore, your daily activities and focus cannot be on fleshly things. You are in the palace to save a nation! You are in the position you are in to reach souls! People will die if you do not fulfill your call!

There are four basic but important principles of the call of being a first lady that I would like to discuss with you:

Principles of the Call: #1 – It is not about you!

Study the life of Esther and see her attitude when accepting the call. The Bible says that she had favor with all of the people because she was not demanding or making all kinds of requests. She took the route of humility and, therefore, was "exalted" by God. The position of first lady is a spiritual position in the

Body of Christ, and you must always remember that you were chosen for God's purpose and not your own personal fulfillment. Like Esther, even in times of what may look like your promotion over your mentor, you must yield, relent, and submit to your spiritual authority.

Principles of the Call: #2 – You must stay humble.

What would have happened if Esther tried to go in front of the king without prayer, without preparation, without favor, and in her own strength? People who do not pray have an independent spirit. Humility is birthed through prayer and consecration. Esther had favor because of her lifestyle of prayer and her lifestyle of humility. Her three-day consecration just activated the power that was already in her.

Principles of the Call: #3 – The call requires a consecrated lifestyle.

A consecrated lifestyle – a separated and set-apart way of living – is necessary to walk in the power that God has for you. Priests, prophets, and all the great men and women of God were called to be separate, even when they were among the people. As a woman in ministry, God requires you to set some relationships apart, some preferences apart, and some time apart to dedicate to His Kingdom and for His glory.

I must again emphasize that Esther was a praying woman, which any call in ministry requires one to be. You will not be effective if you do not pray. Please recognize the damage that will be done if you have a call to save, or speak to, a nation, but you fail to appropriate the power that comes through prayer to fulfill that call.

Principles of the Call: #4 –The call, when fully obeyed, brings authority, power, and influence.

Esther's combination of wisdom and prayer produced a power and influence that set the decree of the Lord. When you, woman of God, operate in wisdom and power in your assigned place, you too will have a level of influence and power unprecedented.

Esther had so much favor that she broke the law and lived! Esther had so much favor that the king offered her half of his kingdom when she broke the law. Esther had so much favor, she set the decree without being king! You see, ladies, every woman of God has the power of influence. If you fully obey, you will be able to set precedents, make decrees, and establish order – all from your own bosom. So, don't get caught up in your title; your title will not give you real power with God, but your submission, obedience, wisdom, and humility will.

When you follow all of the principles of the call, it will automatically lead you to a place of power, authority, and influence. The Bible states that, *"The willing and obedient will eat the good of the land"* (Joshua 1:8). So, there are benefits and blessings that come along with obedience and the attitude of our hearts as we obey our call.

Remember, the servant-leaders will always be the greatest in the sight of God. Decide today that you are more interested in pleasing God than gaining the popularity and admiration of man. Having the mind of Christ, as we serve others, will always lead to a place of exaltation and honor, but first be humble, because *"humility comes before honor"* (Proverbs 15:33). Anyone who has received honor before humility did not receive their honor from God.

CHAPTER THREE

ATTITUDE

"A good name is rather to be chosen than great riches…
loving favor rather than silver and gold."

Proverbs 22:1

The Bible says, ***"Let a man examine himself and see if he be in the faith"*** (II Corinthians 13:5). You may have the religious pedigree to be a first lady and come from a line of ministers. Your mother may have even groomed you to be a first lady. You may have the "first-lady-look" down pat

> *There must be maturity in the first lady that helps her to move on while dealing with issues.*

– the look of elegance and charm – but do you have the servant's character to walk out this gifted position without being a reproach to the Kingdom of God? Your attitude will answer this question. However, I have never known God to give great favor and victory to a person who did not sincerely serve and love.

Attitude and temperament can be synonymous. All of us have weaknesses in our temperaments and in our personalities. However, ministry is no place for a novice. The devil will make mincemeat out of a "rookie" in ministry, because that person has not yet been tried in ministry's fires. There must be maturity in the first lady that helps her to move on while dealing with issues. The first lady must be able to maintain stability in her emotions and in her demeanor while going through various negative situations, like financial problems, marital crises, and all of the other pressures of life.

Some people do not have the maturity to have an argument at home, then step a foot outside of the house and put on another face. They say, "Well, I just can't be phony." No, this is not being phony; this is being mature. Particularly, as the first lady, there is a precedent that is set for other women, which is established by the "set woman" out front. King Ahasuerus and his court understood this principle, which is why Vashti, when she refused to obey the request of her king and husband, was abolished from her place of power. Esther 1:15-18 shows the responsibility and accountability of women in such a position.

ESTHER 1:15-18

15. What shall we do unto the Queen Vashti according to the law, because she hath not performed the commandments of the King Ahasuerus by the chamberlains?

16. And Memucan answered before the king and the princes. <u>Vashti the queen hath not done wrong to the king only, but also to all the princes, and to all the people that are in all the provinces of the King Ahasuerus.</u>

17. For this deed of the queen shall come abroad unto all women, so that they shall despise their husbands in their eyes, when it shall be reported the King Ahasuerus commanded Vashti the queen to be brought in before him, but she came not.

18<u>. Likewise shall the ladies of Persia and Media say this day unto all the king's princes, which have heard of the deed of the queen. Thus shall there arise too much contempt and wrath.</u>

There is a very significant lesson to be learned from Vashti, the first lady of Persia and Media. Although the king's request may have been crude or even inappropriate, the real issue was not in what the king requested – the issue was how Vashti handled his request.

The Bible says in verse 10 of the first chapter of Esther that the king had commanded his chamberlains to bring Vashti before him to show the people and the princes her beauty. Some Bible scholars conclude that he was actually asking for Vashti to dance naked before his guests so that they could see what a fine wife he had! However, it is interesting to note that the inappropriateness of his request is not discussed – just the manner in which it was handled.

The Bible says that a woman who causes shame to her husband is *"like rottenness in his bones"* (Proverbs 12:4). Ladies, you do not ever want to embarrass, shame, or disrespect your mate or any other man of authority publicly, especially as the first lady or as any other ministry role. Why? Because the Scriptures show us that you are setting a precedent in your church and in the Kingdom of how women will relate to their men. Like it or not, the first lady is a position that women will imitate and emulate. You will be held accountable for what the women of your congregation see in your submission, how you talk to your husband, and in your general attitude.

Vashti could have successfully handled this situation differently, by at least coming to the king and pleading out of the godly influence that God has given all women. All women have the power of persuasion. Search the Scriptures and see how, from Genesis to Revelation, women have persuaded men. Eve persuaded Adam to do something God Himself told him not to do, and Adam was not confused about God's direction. Delilah persuaded Sampson after countless times of being tricked. (You would have thought he would not have fallen for that one!) Esther persuaded Ahasuerus. The persistent woman in Luke 18:1-8 persuaded the judge. Mary persuaded Jesus to turn water into wine when He told her, *"My time hath not yet come."* Our Lord and Savior was persuaded by a woman! So ladies, use your God-given power.

Unfortunately, Vashti chose to have a poor attitude, walk in the flesh, and show the king that he did not control her. So it cost her the throne, her destiny, and her calling. **The cost of a bad attitude can be very high!**

If you have the Word of the Lord in you and if you have any kind of relationship with the Lord that really matters to you, then you will do anything to stay connected to God.

Apostle Paul said, *"I will let nothing separate me from the love of God."* Nothing means nothing! It means that you will not tolerate someone mistreating you; you will not put up with someone hurting you; you will not allow any devil from hell to get you out of God's presence and prevent you from being righteous before Him.

You must remember that as a first lady and co-laborer with your spouse, it means something to be a watchman over the souls of God's people. God will not allow you to continually abuse or mislead His sheep.

> *There is no such thing as a first lady with a bad attitude.*

Did not God ask Saul of Tarsus: *"Saul, Saul, why persecuteth thou me?"* Saul did not touch the Lord physically, but in touching His children, he was persecuting God.

If your attitude is bad, it cancels you out from walking in this calling. There is no such thing as a first lady (who is really one) with a bad attitude. We have a lot of women who want to climb up the spiritual ladder of success, who think they are ready to pastor, or ready to preach the Gospel, but it first begins with your self-examination.

Being the pastor's wife, a pastor, or in any position in ministry is a "fishbowl" lifestyle. There is no room for mistakes. You may ask, "How can I be this perfect person?" I know it is impossible to be perfect (even though we strive for perfection), but if your attitude is right, people do not always expect perfection from you. When you are arrogant, you make people beat you up; you make people talk about you. People look to find things wrong about you, just because of your arrogance.

Your attitude is often reflected in how much you smile. I believe that most women who do not smile are arrogant or they have some "head" (psychological) problems. I believe if other people are not smiling, you ought to give them yours. A smile disarms a lot of people. The prettiest smile ought to be on the face of the first lady. Even if you have a grumpy husband, if you maintain a smile, the people will think, "He can't be so bad – look at his wife!" However, if both of you are grumpy, people will be afraid to approach you. When you think about how many people are dependent upon you to fulfill the role of a godly, caring, loving, supportive person, and how you can mess up that image, you will find the reserve and intestinal fortitude to reach down and grab a smile — even when you do not feel like it. You can find joy because you are a child of God and because you are responsible for setting the precedent.

My first wife, Denise, and I had some of our worst arguments before we got to church and then after we left out of church. That "last-word" demon will show up in the mouth of an immature person (both male and female), I promise you. When your attitude is bad, you will think first and last about yourself. You will not even care what people's opinions are about you. However, when you are in ministry, you live and die by public opinion.

You may say, "Well, I don't care." That shows signs of pride, immaturity, and irresponsibility. You do not need to be in ministry. You will not go far or be successful in anything with that kind of attitude.

You need an attitude check every day. Not selfishness, but self*less*ness is the order of the day, and is not hard when you are true servants of God.

> *When you come into God's presence, you cannot stay the same; you cannot continue to sin and displease Him.*

11

An irritable attitude reflects a lack of a prayer life. You cannot convince me that you have any kind of decent prayer life or that you are in the face of God daily, when you consistently have such an ugly disposition. When you come into God's presence, you cannot stay the same; you cannot continue to sin and displease Him. You cannot stay before God and He not deal with you. Anybody who is mean, unfriendly, cantankerous, and critical, and claims to have a word from the Lord, emphatically letting you know about the hours they spent in prayer, is a liar!

All of us have issues in our lives that are unpleasant. Mature people know how to handle daily dilemmas without bringing everybody into their conflict.

A first lady must be very careful because, regardless of how anointed your husband is, your attitude can destroy everything God is trying to build. If you love God, you should never do anything negative, especially in terms of embarrassing your husband. (Remember what Solomon said about a woman embarrassing her husband being like rottenness in his bones.) You should never do anything that would embarrass your husband publicly. You cannot ever justify that. Never! (Remember Vashti?) Neither can the man be justified about embarrassing his wife in public, for that matter. Neither of you should ever disrespect one another in a public place and justify why you had to "go off," bringing humiliation to the House of God, to the call of God, and to the Word of God. You cannot justify it one bit!

You must understand that you have one chance to make a first impression. If you lose that image of being a godly first lady, it will be like letting go of feathers on top of a mountain and trying to retrieve them. The positive image of you will be gone forever. Think about some well-known first ladies in ministry whose images have been tarnished; see if they can ever be respected as godly first ladies again. Never. Ever.

When you really love God, you ask Him before you do or say anything: "Lord, will this hurt the church? Will this hurt the saints? Will I hurt You if I do or say this?" When you really love God, there are things you do not stoop to do because of the place you are in. ***To whom much is given, much is required*** (Luke 12:48 paraphrased). First ladies are given much authority, much power, many benefits, and honor. You cannot forget that the flipside of all of that is a

> *When you really love God, there are things you do not stoop to do because of the place you are in.*

requirement of much sacrifice, much dying to self, much humility, much wisdom, and much patience.

I go across the country and what I see in terms of first ladies stinks! It seems as if no one is talking to these ladies about their attitude.

Now, I know some of you ladies out there may be thinking right about now that, "Of course, as a man, you are just seeing one side." I do want to acknowledge another side to the first lady dilemma: An often-common reason for first ladies with bad attitudes is unsupportive husbands. I say to the men from my pulpit, "When you mess with my wife, you are messing with me." My former wife, Denise, was co-pastor, but even if she were not co-pastor, I would still tell them, "You are still messing with me." If someone has a problem with my woman, come talk to me; but do not get up in my woman's face and do not even think about disrespecting her.

Sadly, many women do not have the support they need from their husbands. Could it be that the husbands are jealous of the call on their wives' life? Could it be that she is more disciplined to pray, to fast, consecrate, and study the Word of God? Could it be that she has the mouth of wisdom? Could it be that the husband may not like the attention the wife is getting in the church? Could it be the obvious, that the wife is the most anointed and so more people show up to listen to her than the pastor? I have to admit that, unfortunately, I have seen all of the above scenarios. Countless times, quite frankly, there has been a greater anointing on the woman of God than on her mate, and it usually results in a negative attitude in that woman, unless she is mature, steadfast, and grounded in the Word of God.

If you are one of those women in this type of situation, let me tell you: You still have a responsibility to remain godly and not allow the kingdom of God to be blasphemed because of you.

I recognize that it is a very hard situation. However, you must understand that through your blamelessness before God, He will be able to work on your behalf and He will fix the problem. If you allow yourself to have anxiety, become frustrated, and act out of character, you have then disqualified yourself from the Divine Intervention of God. But, when you remain blameless, your assured victory is in store (Proverbs 11:6). To believe that anyone can keep you from your purpose and destiny in God is to place them at a higher level than God. As long as you obey what He says, know that your purpose will be fulfilled!

The growth of my church in the early years was due largely to my wife, who was visibly out front, who other women looked at and said, "That's what I need to be like." I am extremely blessed by how God used Denise in that way.

Was Denise a perfect woman? No. She was not perfect. You are not going to live a perfect life, but you had better be striving for it. People know when you are trying, sisters. Part of your attitude ought to be that of humility. It is nice to be important, but it is more important to be nice.

Isaiah 1:19 says, ***"If you are willing and obedient, you will eat the good of the land."*** This denotes more than just your physical actions of obedience. It emphasizes that both the action and the attitude are necessary for you to obtain the "good success" – the perfect will that God has for your marriage, your ministry, and your money.

Even as God may have blessed all of these areas in your life, when you look into the mirror of God, you better not begin to see yourself as a "hotshot" or somebody just so anointed above the rest. Do not allow people, things, accolades, or notoriety to mess you up. People can start whispering things in your ear, and before you know it,

> *Your name, your gift, your connections, or your good looks may get you through the door, but only character will keep you there.*

you start thinking you are who the people say you are. Never forget this very important fact: The same people who said, "Hosanna," a couple of days later said "Crucify Him."

Your name, your gift, your connections, or your good looks may get you through the door, but only character will keep you there. You can teach what you know, but you will produce what you are. People will come to your church because of what you project; but when they ultimately see what you are, they will leave. Nothing will send people out of the door quicker than seeing a first lady who is arrogant and whose attitude stinks. I know several pastors whose churches have emptied out because of the bad attitude of the first lady.

Keep your attitude in check by maintaining a consistent prayer life and staying in submission to your husband. Your attitude will also stay in check if you submit yourself to other godly women who have gone through what you have to go through and who have been examples of virtuous women.

Most of us really do not like being accountable to other people, because we really do not want to be corrected. Every first lady needs another seasoned first lady to *"teach her to be sober, to love her husband, and to love her children"* (Titus 2:4). Note that Paul acknowledged that there are some things that **women need to teach women**.

> *You can teach what you know, but you will produce who you are.*

We all too often call people who agree with us and tell us all good things our "friends," while the people whom God sent into our lives to tell us the truth become the "enemy." You need to find yourself a real friend – a woman of God who will teach you and train you like Naomi schooled Ruth. Your submission to a woman such as this will lead you right into your place of prosperity, peace, and provision.

Chapter Four

APPEARANCE

*"It came to pass on the third day, that Esther put on
her royal apparel and stood in the inner court...."*

Esther 5:1

As a first lady and as a leader who represents the authority of God, it is imperative that you understand what Esther understood about her role as a first lady. Since you are the chosen and very elect of God, you have a higher level of expectation, sacrifice, and commitment that must be demonstrated, not just in prayer and consecration, but also in your appearance. You see, you too are in the "inner court" of the King. You represent His headship and His authority and there is royal apparel that accompanies the inner court.

All throughout Scripture, there are indications of the importance of the garments worn by the priests and those in positions of authority. God commissioned Moses to sanctify the garments of Aaron and his sons. Esther knew to wear her royal apparel in the inner court. When Joseph was promoted to second in command, Pharaoh immediately *put him in vestures of fine linen.*

> *We have a responsibility and accountability to reflect modesty, integrity, temperance, and holiness, even in our dress.*

You must understand that just as in the days of old, your attire prophesies to your authority. Beggars wore the garments of beggars; whores the garments of whores; and queens the apparel of royalty.

It is a travesty that we do not recognize today the significance of our garments as men and women of God. We have a responsibility and accountability to reflect modesty, integrity, temperance, and holiness, even in our dress.

Understand that you are dealing with a very critical public. Although we cannot live our lives to please men, we are nonetheless charged not to offend those who are weak. Therefore, we must use wisdom concerning our dress, basing it on our audience. For example, wearing a pantsuit to a speaking engagement to minister would be something that you would need to know will not be an offense to your audience. Also, being overly "flashy" or overdressing may cause schism and set a poor example for the other women in the church.

First ladies, in particular, should be careful about their dress, because they are the trendsetters among the women in the church. Whatever the "look" the first lady sets will be the "look" of the entire church. If the first lady starts whacking her hair off, you will have a church full of shorthaired women. If the first lady wears pants to church, then so will the rest of the women.

Women look to the first lady to determine the standard or norm. Therefore, you must be particularly careful not to wear clothing, makeup, or jewelry that appears carnal and inappropriate for a church setting.

I have been appalled while going across the country and seeing the apparel of some of the first ladies. Even the world understands that a dress code is necessary to maintain a professional environment. Do you not know that there is a certain dress code that must be maintained to keep a holy environment?

Some of what I am referring to relates to just being a lady. My mother would tell my sisters to take precautionary measures not to expose themselves or their undergarments if they are wearing a low-cut top. Under those circumstances, she taught them to put their hand over their chest if leaning forward. It is all about having tact, having poise, and having charm. Why, because you are going to produce after your own example. So, you cannot wear anything and everything.

You must be honest with yourself. If you are large in a certain area, be honest with yourself. Too many ladies are in denial. When you wear clothes so tight that they look like they are sprayed on your body, you are in denial. When any part of your clothing brings attention to any specific part of your body, you are inappropriately dressed. You do not want to bring attention to yourself because then the Christ that is inside of you is being overshadowed by your appearance.

A first lady should never be caught with splits that are all the way up her dress or with cleavage showing. Just look at the first lady of our nation and get a revelation of the importance of dress. You will never see the first lady in anything remotely inappropriate. Why? Because she knows that her office demands respect, and what she wears is a reflection of her position.

Another aspect of your appearance is not just your dress, but also your countenance. Although I have already addressed attitude in Chapter Two, I thought it must be reemphasized that your appearance includes your countenance, which is defined as expression. The look on your face, whether it is one of joy or the lack thereof, is just as much a part of your appearance, if not the most important part. As with the clothing, the precedent that you set will be the standard of your church.

As a leader and as the leading example to the women of God, you must demonstrate the fruit of joy in your life. Dress codes were once enforced in the church as a religious constriction to enslave women. In response to these constrictions, we now see rebellious dressing in the church. At one time, pantsuits were not allowed in the church. However, there is nothing wrong with pantsuits, except when they are worn with the pants fitting too tight. It then becomes a stumbling block for some men. Tastefully appropriate is to have your jacket cover your rear parts.

As a leader and as the leading example to the women of God, you must be a demonstrator of the fruit of joy in your life – even in your appearance.

CHAPTER FIVE

FAMILY

"Her husband doth trust safely in her…her
children rise up and call her blessed."

Proverbs 31:11, 28

God is a family man. The whole creation began as a family and it is going to end with family. God created the family as the natural representation and vehicle by which we gain our revelation, appreciation, and definition of love, support, respect, authority, obedience, and character. It is the family that forms the community and church; and the communities formulate cities; and the cities make up nations.

It is the responsibility of the woman of the house to ensure that she *"**builds up her house**,"* and creates an environment that is healthy, productive, God-fearing, and loving. The woman is the critical component of every house and "as it is in the natural," God utilizes the biological family to show us the spiritual parallel of His Divine Order.

The first lady is also the God-ordained "builder" of the spiritual house. Building up the house refers to making sure that everything and everyone, every activity and every person within the house is in alignment with "building" or edification, construction, and positive development.

The Bible clearly states that, *"**every wise woman buildeth up her house**."* So, we know that any woman, any first lady who does not edify her husband, her children, and any others who make up her house is a foolish woman and will destroy the house with her own hands.

The same principle applies to the first lady as the builder of your church. As the "mother" of the house, you are more sensitive in many areas to the needs of the house than your spouse is. The first lady must perpetuate family. I believe that is the first lady's main responsibility in the House of the Lord – to make sure the holistic family is ministered to.

Furthermore, I believe it is the first lady's job to institute some ministries in the church to which the man just does not have the sensitivity or the wisdom.

It is the first lady who makes sure there is a nursery. What does a man know about having Pampers and toys in stock? It is the first lady's job because she is a mother and she knows the needs of the family. She knows things the man does not and thinks about things that he does not.

For example, when trying to decide where the nursery should be in your beautiful new building, your spouse may choose the room in the back of the church by the exit door. However, the first lady would know that that room would not suffice, because of the draft coming through the door and the effect that the draft would have on the children, creating susceptibility to colds, flu, and other ailments.

It is also important that the first lady does not have the attitude of a "doormat" (someone everyone steps on). The first lady needs to speak up and not just be a knot on a log or just "the pastor's wife."

The first lady brings value to the importance of making sure holistically that every facet of the church appeals to a specific part of the family. She must have sensitivity for the men, women, and children.

Let's look at I Timothy 3:1-2 to get a clear picture of how God utilizes your "family life" to determine your ability to qualify for the spiritual parenting of His people.

"This is a faithful saying: If a man desires the position of a bishop, he desires a good work. A bishop then must be blameless, the husband of <u>one wife</u>, temperate, sober-minded, of good behavior, hospitable, and able to teach."

It is quite clear that God utilizes one's everyday lifestyle, family structure, and marriage as a prophetic symbol and a barometer of their readiness to oversee His house. The principal message of this Scripture is that the way we live daily in our homes as spouses, our habits, and our ability to even rule our own house and our own children will speak volumes about where we are in God, in relation to the level of maturity, wisdom, and responsibility that also comes with such a position of authority.

As Apostle Paul was talking to the man, he was also outlining the responsibilities of

> *The mother of every house, whether natural or spiritual, must have a real presence in order for that house to have the order that God has ordained.*

the first ladies. How do I know this? Because some of the key elements that must be in order, "having children in subjection," and given to hospitality, are usually responsibilities and giftings that God has placed within the woman.

The mother of every house, whether natural or spiritual, must have a real presence in order for that house to have the order that God has ordained. A mother's heart must be in the house of God to bring balance. This is also what Paul is saying to the first ladies: "Help out your husband in the area of being patient, so he won't be a brawler. How many husbands have wives who will pull them to the side and say, "Honey, don't do that; don't say that"? This is what a wife does. This is also what the first lady should do.

You can tell when the first lady does not have a voice in the church. When there is a ministry where there is a woman who has a voice, there is balance, sensitivity, and creativity in the church. If the husband is not careful, he will have everything so regimented that the women many times will not be able to relate or have an outlet to be the creative vessels and builders that God has called them to be. She will not have the freedom to be ministered to on the level that is necessary to grow, mature, and become whole. There are instances when the children will suffer along with the mother. It will eventually spill over to the church and cause the church to "die out," because the pastor lacks sensitivity to the youth and does not recognize the changing of the times.

As the first lady and the "role model mother" of the church, the image that you project will be the image that you will draw. If you project an independent, non-submissive, cantankerous wife and mother image, you will draw the same type of individuals. You will be held accountable by God for the image that you project to His sheep.

The first lady (or co-pastor, etc.) must be submissive and understand parameters. If you do not understand these areas, you should not be in ministry.

Spiritual authority says that the man is the "head of the house." The wife is the builder, but the husband is the head. Now, I do recognize for some spiritual houses, the order may differ; but regardless of titles between a husband and wife, at home the man is the head! God really does not use anyone who does not follow orders, because this would set the precedent of disorder and unruliness in a house. Since the wife sets the precedent in the house, you have the greater level of responsibility and the greater condemnation.

I must stop here to say this: As much as you have a responsibility in the church, your first responsibility is with your family. Often, as ministries grow, husbands and wives begin to neglect one another and their children in the effort of trying to be "successful" in ministry. It is important to always remember according to I Timothy (paraphrased), "Your family's success precedes your ministry's success (when you do it God's way)." You are a wife first, then a mother, and lastly, first lady.

Many first ladies make the mistake of forgetting that they are married first. Whether the cause of abandoning the marriage is the church or the children, neglect of your spouse is wrong. If you

> *Take care of your husband and do not take him for granted.*

have not prepared his dinner, or your home is nasty, or you did not make love to him last night like you promised, or things that he asked you to do are not done, or you drove all of the gas out of his car, or you did not make the bank deposit because you did not have time – honey, you are out of order!

Take care of your man and do not take him for granted. Say, "Honey, is there something I need to do? Am I missing something here?" Make sure the needs of your spouse are being met.

I owe a lot to my first wife, Denise, in learning about myself and realizing my own needs. You would be surprised, ladies, what an impact your support, love, and kindness will do for your mate. I learned from Denise what kind of man I was. And in the process of her love, she showed me she was the one I needed. She was a cheerleader and clearly admired me as a man.

We need first ladies today who are going to learn how to admire men again. People all across the country would say to me, "I just love to watch your wife when you are preaching. She just sits there and smiles. She really loves you." I needed that. It spoiled me through the years, but it taught me that I needed someone who loved me and admired me.

Ephesians 5:33 says, ***"And the wife, see that she reverences her husband."*** To reverence means to be in awe of, to revere, to respect, and to pay homage to. God says for you to see to it that you do this.

There are too many first ladies and women in ministry who do not recognize the importance of admiring their husbands. It does not just impact him tremendously, but it impacts your children, the house of God, and, also, whether or not the church grows.

There are many women in ministry with many issues concerning their husbands. Trust me, ladies, those issues will eventually come out of your mouth as well as be obvious in your body language. It is going to come out in the way you <u>do not</u> support him. People can tell when a husband and wife love, honor, and respect one another. It is the little things and *"the little foxes that spoil the vine"* (Song of Solomon 2:15).

Ladies, please understand how much of an important factor you are in the growth of your mate and in the growth of the church. As your spouse is inspired to do more for God, it is helpful when he receives your encouragement from home to be more anointed. Ultimately, the congregation becomes the recipient of that anointing. The people will be blessed, and be taught; they will receive their deliverance and grow by leaps and bounds. This will cause your ministry not only to grow but, more importantly, to be effective. So, if I know this, I know Satan knows this too, and he must not be allowed access to destroy what God is trying to build.

I know what some of you are thinking: "Apostle Turner, you do not know who I am living with! I cannot find anything to admire about him right now." Well, I say to you that you are going to have to "call those things that be not as though they were." I know it is not easy and it takes endurance; but the reality of your relationship with God is that no matter how bad we believe our spouses are, when we go to God, He is always going to show you – not your spouse, but you!

Some of you may have a hard time admiring your husband because you are so angry with him. You still haven't gotten over the summer of 1942. If that is the case, you have now entered into areas of pride, which leads you to become bitter. And, eventually, if you are not careful, the bitterness will *"dry the bones"* (Proverbs 17:22) – in other words, cause sickness and disease – and hand you over to death! So, for your own good, you must put away your pride, anger, and unforgiveness, and see your husband as God sees him, loving him unconditionally and building him up.

For many of you, it is this same unforgiveness, anger, and disappointment that has you unable to submit to your spouse. Well, I am telling you right now that you have already cancelled your date with destiny, unless you can walk in forgiveness. It is important to love your husband unconditionally, and if nobody else admires him, he needs to know that he has your admiration.

Satan knows that if he can tear up your marriage, he can also destroy your family, and then bring destruction to his ultimate enemy – the church. You cannot be ignorant of Satan's devices. Your battle begins and ends in your house. This is why the enemy fights your marriage, tooth and nail. He particularly fights your marriage bed – the place of restoration, procreation, and (in Jesus's name!) recreation. Have you taken a look at the statistics of Christian marriages lately? Did you know that the divorce rate among Christians is higher than that of the world? Have you heard about the countless divorces among the five-fold ministry officers?

> *You cannot be ignorant of Satan's devices. Your battle begins and ends in your house.*

Now, let's test your marriage by allowing me to give you a simple test. This is the test: What is the state of your marriage bed? It's as plain as that, because if you were to tell me the state of your marriage bed, I can tell you the state of your marriage. You say there is no marriage bed? I say there is no marriage. You say you have a great marriage bed? I say you have a great marriage.

Through a successful sex life, God has designed that you not just bond physically, but emotionally as well. That is why Solomon warned that physical relations with women other than your wife would destroy your own soul (Proverbs 6:32). What makes up the soul? The soul is made up of your mind, your will, and your emotions. So, what does the frequent bonding with the wife produce? It produces a couple that not only becomes physically one, but a couple that starts thinking alike, finishing one another's sentences, and being on one accord. How do you develop this? It is not in the spirit, sister; it's in the bed.

Once again, that is why the Bible says that when a man has sex with a woman outside of marriage, he destroys his own soul. When a man makes love to a woman, he is releasing things not only out of his body, but also out of his mind, out of his soul, and out of his spirit. Could the lack of "coming together" be the reason why you and your spouse are not on one accord?

God has fixed it so that you are supposed to be the only person who can legally tap into the fullness of your mate's anointing. This is an awesome state of being, by which you are enabled to fully help your husband.

God also uses the marriage bed to replenish your energy. This is why I believe more than anything that every pastor (whether male or female) should be married. Why, because your place of prayer (particularly with men) and your coming together with your spouse strengthens you. When a man is properly encouraged, loved, affirmed, liked, and admired by his wife, there is nothing he feels he cannot do. When the opposite occurs, there is nothing he feels he can do. I believe that the lack of refreshing and inspiration is, yes, at the feet of Jesus, and the rest is in the marriage bed.

Satan has cleverly utilized his knowledge of the power of the marriage bed to get couples to argue, fight, and remain separate; and the first thing that suffers is their intimacy. Quite frankly, I have encountered too many first ladies who, because of their immaturity and lack of wisdom in this area, have made their husbands open prey for the devil. Although their "holding back" on their husbands did not give their husbands an excuse to sin, I believe that God also holds the wife accountable for being rebellious and clearly defying God's commandment concerning husbands and wives: Their bodies no longer belong to themselves but to each other.

We must not withhold our marital responsibilities from one another. There is no "real" reason to justify denying your spouse.

Do you have an affectionate husband? If you do, he demands attention. God has placed you with that man to take care of him, love him, and support him.

You cannot be doing anything great in the Kingdom of God if your house is neglected. Do not give the devil "a place" in your house, in your marriage, and in your children.

I have seen an unfortunate number of wives who have not accepted their responsibilities for their families and are paying the price for their lack of sensitivity to their family's needs. Too many wives are destroying their marriages and, ultimately, their families because they do not understand both the natural and spiritual implications of maintaining healthy and consistent intimacy with their spouses. The relationship between you, your spouse, and God affect the entire family.

Ladies, you are on display as a first lady (or pastor), and not only are the people watching every move you make, but God holds you even more accountable as a teacher: ***"Thou that teachest one not to steal...dost thou steal?"***

(Romans 2:21 paraphrased). If you have the gift of prophecy and you are exhorting women to live for God, obey God, submit and praise God in spite of their circumstances, you better make sure that you are the first partaker of everything that you are exhorting the saints to do.

I was the overseer of a ministry for women. The women who headed that ministry would be on the radio, telling women to submit and love their husbands. Yet, they were two of the meanest women I have ever met. It would knock my socks off listening to them tell women to do what they were not willing to do themselves. As their overseer, I had to address the situation and correct their constant badgering of the ladies in their audience, as well as remind them of their responsibility to actively seek to live what they preach. When you have godly integrity, your words and your deeds match. If they don't, God will not honor what comes out of your mouth.

Needless to say, my relationship with those women was over after that conversation, and their ministry did not last long, since their message was not valid. It was not invalid because the Scriptures they quoted weren't true. Yes, they quoted the Scriptures accurately. However, their ministry was not valid because there was no power behind the ministry: These vessels were operating out of the "letter" of the Word (or out of legalism), instead of the "spirit" of the Word. You can only get the results of the anointing when the Spirit has been allowed to have liberty in you.

Your children will also speak of your effectiveness as a mother and builder of the home. We all know that most of the time, the end is better than the beginning when raising children; furthermore, raising children will have its ups and downs.

Of course, I am not saying that your family should or will be perfect. However, because of your spiritual position and Satan wanting to embarrass and destroy you, knowing how critical you are, I cannot stress enough that you must not be ignorant of his devices. The enemy will always try to attack you at the weakest links, which are oftentimes our children.

I have nine children and, believe me, every day the enemy is attempting to come through one of them or the other. Knowing that my wife's Achilles' heel is her children, we have had to strictly monitor their associations, their activities, and their lives. My wife and I spend a lot of time on the road, and we have three adults who help us to chaperone and escort our children everywhere they need to go. Besides prayer and speaking the

Word of the Lord over their lives, we have had to solicit the help of our families and the saints to ensure that they do not get lost in the shuffle and that their physical, emotional, and spiritual needs are being attended to and met.

The woman, as the builder of the house, must always take "inspections" of her children and determine: Are they respectful? Do they dress respectfully? Are they representing the principles that we teach? Are they courteous, responsible? Do they have a foundation of the Word built inside of them? As you teach, train, love, correct, and discipline your children, despite what bumps may occur along the road, in the end, they will *"rise up and call you blessed."*

About now, I know you may be thinking, "Okay, I know what I am supposed to be to my husband; I know what my responsibilities are as a mother; but what about me? Am I not part of the family? Do I not deserve

> *People who value themselves are going to take care of themselves.*

a rest?" Well, the answer is "Yes, you most certainly do!" I always advise parents that as much as any husband and wife love their children, and as much as they love their family, they need to plan and take time for themselves. You need to come *apart* before you come *a part*!

Do not allow your family and the ministry to consume you to the point that you are tired and cantankerous. It is hard to be spiritual when you are tired. Satan loves to attack tired people. You must, as a wife and mother, firstly value yourself and your role in your home and in the ministry. People who value themselves are going to take care of themselves. Take time out daily for "quiet time." Set priorities in ministry and know that you cannot accomplish everything in one day. You will not last long in ministry if you do not know how to adjust. What worked last week may not work today. Do your best...and then you rest.

Do not allow family, friends, or the saints to make you feel guilty about your commitment to your family, your children, and yourself. No one has the right to demand that you not be a wife to your husband, a mother to your children, or value yourself. It would be sad to live life having a great church, but never having a great home to go to when church is over.

Remember your spiritual mother, Sarah, who had a voice with her spouse; she was submitted to her husband, and she made sure to look out for her child.

"Like Sarah who obeyed Abraham and called him her master, you are her daughters, if you do what is right, and do not give way to fear." (NIV – I Peter 3:6)

Purpose in your heart today to be a daughter of Sarah and do what is right!

CHAPTER SIX

WITNESS

"Giving no offense in anything, that the ministry be not blamed."

II Corinthians 6:3

We are the keyhole through which people see Christ. We must make sure that whatever we do, we are guarding our witness. Particularly as church leaders and members of the five-fold ministry offices, we have a responsibility to "die to ourselves" at an even greater level; because we will often set the precedent for our local church, cities, and for those of us with national and international influence, nations. Have you been guarding your witness in conversation, attitude, appearance, and associations? If you don't invite it, you won't have to entertain it!

There are many definitions and interpretations of what it means to "be separate and come out from among them." This has also been a much-debated topic. I am not advocating being reclusive, arrogant, and "holier than thou." (We all know that Jesus had times when He ate with sinners and did some very unorthodox things in spreading the Gospel.) So, let me begin by saying that I am not referring to such specific situations where we are clearly led by the Spirit of God to minister to, or interact with, people who may have questionable lives, when I say "be separate." Yet, I am referring to our everyday, consistent lifestyle of associations, habits, attitudes, appearances, and conversations.

Paul said to the Roman church, ***"For the name of the Lord is evil spoken of among the heathen because of you."*** We must remember that we still do have accountability as representatives of Christ to ***"abstain from all appearance of evil"*** and to protect our witness as being people who walk in truth, love, and integrity.

Unfortunately, as Christian leaders, whatever you do, people – your congregation, your city – will blame the church for your personal mistakes. You must keep that in mind as you make decisions that involve business associates and everything else that you do. You are what you hang around.

Some of you are suffering right now from innocently entering into some situations that you had no idea would blow up in your face and cause reproach for you, your family, your church, and ultimately the Kingdom of God. You need to always keep in mind that the devil wants to embarrass the House of God. He is waiting to find something to go to God on you about. That is why he is called "the accuser of the brethren." He wants to be able to accuse you of evil, deception, wrong associations, and bad attitudes. You need to aspire to be like Jesus, so that when the devil comes, there will be nothing found in you.

Apostolic wisdom says, "If you want to know what you look like, look at your friends. If you want to know what you are going to become, look at your leaders."

Galatians 5:19 says, ***"Now, the works of the flesh are manifest which are these: adultery, fornication, uncleanness, lasciviousness, idolatry...."*** Obviously, these are all things that should not once be named among us as Christians and, particularly, leadership. However, far too often, not only has one been named among the five-fold ministers and first ladies, but <u>all</u> of the above!

Lasciviousness is living a lifestyle so carnal that people cannot see Christ because they are looking at so much of you. You can be lascivious in your conversation, your dress, and/or your priorities.

I have experienced far too many first ladies and pastors whose primary conversation was their latest shopping spree, their next shopping spree, or what they were believing (by "faith," of course) for God to do for them, which usually amounted to more of a personal focus than one on the Kingdom. Of course, I am not saying that we are not to believe God for the best and for things we desire. **However, the current trend has produced a generation of people who have really disguised the "American Dream" under the cloak of "faith" and have abandoned the Great Commission.**

Faith for big houses, expensive cars, and six-digit incomes is common in the Kingdom, but where is the hunger for souls and the outreach ministries? Too many conferences and events have been directed at getting the house packed in and inviting speakers who can raise the most money. What happened to trying to reach the lost and ministering to the poor?

Decked out in St. John suits and five-carat diamonds, much of the "faith" of the Christian leadership has been extended toward the next Mercedes-Benz and the next house. Has anyone stopped to think what kind of image and witness is being projected? Do you have any idea what kind of people you are attracting and the underlying motives of many of the people who are sitting in the church today? Things have their place, but they are not priority.

We must preach, teach, and exhibit a balanced Gospel and keep Christ and His Kingdom's purposes before people, and not our own purposes. Even the world understands this principle for their leadership, which is why the president and his family know they cannot flaunt their wealth; they must be discreet, they must be discreet in their associations, and they cannot wear just anything that they want to wear. The world seems to understand this – dressing for success – but the saints think, "That's bondage." No, that is wisdom, that is maturity, that is accountability, and that is responsibility.

Furthermore, anyone who is not willing or able to step up to this responsibility need not place themselves in any position of leadership or responsibility where people will be influenced by you or looking to your lifestyle as a role model. If you do not want to make those adjustments, you do not need to be in ministry.

The first lady of our country understands that for her "witness," she cannot wear everything. Yet, I have seen too many sensually dressed first ladies in the Kingdom of God. Yes, you may be shapely and voluptuous, but tight and clingy clothes, splits, see-through blouses, and low-plunging necklines have no place for women in ministry. The first lady should never be found in clothing that compromises her witness and disrespects her husband. Read what Apostle Paul said about how God would handle lasciviousness in II Corinthians 12:19-21.

I remember a story about a first lady who attended a conference with her husband. The conference was for a few days, and her husband was the main speaker. She never came to any of the meetings until the last night they were there. On the last night of her husband's engagement, she came to service dressed in tight leopard pants, with an attitude to match. Needless to say, the focus and topic of that evening was not the Word or the move of the Spirit; it was the audacities of the first lady to, firstly, not attend any of the services and then, when she did come, to show up looking like a "hooker." Ladies, something as simple as your clothing can cause people to lose respect for you as a woman of God, and that is not worth the contentiousness that it may cause.

You also must be cognizant of the beliefs of the people to whom you may be ministering. If it "offends your brother," you should stay away from it. Today, it is common for many women to minister in pants. However, if the church or ministry group that has sponsored your engagement is offended by that, you need to know that, and honor that and not be too prideful to make the adjustment. Remember, it is not about you.

The Bible instructs us not to offend our brothers, and to stay away from things that would cause those who are weak to backslide. There are too many ministers and first ladies who do not believe they need to make adjustments. Instead, they demand that everyone else adjusts to them.

I know many first ladies who go around telling their husbands' business – not only first ladies, but women in ministry. If that is you, sisters, then you have become a tool of the devil, betraying the trust of your husband, leadership, overseer, or whomever God has placed in your life as a spiritual authority. The devil will make sure your commentary gets back to the person that you have talked about so that he can accuse you of "causing discord among the brethren (which, by the way, is something that God hates).

> *You must remember that we have been called to cover and not uncover. It's a "covering" and not a "cover-up."*

You must remember that you have been called to cover and not uncover. Praise in public; rebuke in private. Even if your mate upsets you before church starts, you are uplifting him as a man of God whenever you are before the saints. This is not a cover-up; it is a covering. This is maturity and it is a representation of a wise woman.

Am I saying that you pretend problems are not there? No. Am I saying you do not deal with those problems? No. I am saying that you must be in order by only submitting your problems to those who are the ordained authorities in your life, such as your overseer – not your girlfriends or your shopping buddies.

It is very important that you protect the witness of the Kingdom. Yet, not only do you protect the witness of the Kingdom, but also you must protect the witness of your spouse, your family, and your ministry. Again, I must stress that I am not saying not to deal with the issues; I am saying to deal with them in an orderly, respectful manner, protecting your witness and the witness of the Kingdom.

We must grow up as leaders and realize that "to whom much is given, much is required." God requires sacrifice, accountability, and responsibility for His leaders. Your problems are not that important that you ever have the right to offend those people who look to you for leadership and maturity. Whatever you may be going through, you have a responsibility to keep your attitude, conversation, and actions pure so that you will not be an embarrassment to the Kingdom of God. If you cannot do that, you are not ready for ministry. You cannot get so angry with people that they see you upset; you should not walk out of a service or "go off" on someone who may have done something to you. Why, because it oversteps the boundaries of a leader and a person who has been chosen by God to be an example to His people.

Another mistake I have seen many women in ministry make is that they have attempted to be friends with the saints in the church, which ultimately leads to compromising their witness. People tend to lose respect for you when they become common with you. All of us have personal issues or quirks that often will be misunderstood, judged, and criticized by the "average" Christian, which is why you need not have any average Christians in your inner circle. You cannot be naïve about this. I know you are trying to be nice and approachable, and you can be that and still use wisdom. Even the world tells you "familiarity breeds contempt." People lose respect for you, the closer you get to them. They will begin to say and do things that they normally would not say or do. They will begin to see you as their "buddy," and, eventually, see you as being on the same level as they are.

There are people who want to get close to you only to get in your business. It is not because they want to serve you, or because God led them. Honey, they are just trying to get in your business. They want to know how much money you make, what kind of house you live in, whether your children are on the ministry payroll, etc. You must understand these things and know how to feed people with a "long-handled" spoon; otherwise, you are going to experience some things that could eventually damage your ministry.

I must admit that I have not always adhered to this and I have suffered the consequences of it. I have found that no matter what you are going through, you must keep yourself in check. I have taken people into "my bosom" who really never had the character to be there. I have had some very overwhelming circumstances that I am sure most of you would agree could make anyone "snap."

I lost my first wife of twenty years. Then, I went through a divorce. My leadership had begun to attempt to tear up the church while I was grieving. The church suffered from this, as well as from many other issues. Needless to say, I was angry. During the course of all of this, I said some things that I regret saying. I honestly do not even remember all that I said and did, because I was just that "out of it" during that season. Adding to the situation, I was surrounded by people with wrong motives, people who were immature, and people never ordained to be a part of my ministry – much less part of my inner circle.

I have come to realize now, however, that I really should not have been in the pulpit. I should have taken some time off. I should have allowed myself to receive ministry, instead of pressing myself to minister in my condition. I should have been surrounded by people with the character of Christ, to love and cover.

This is why I plead with you not to make the same mistake that I did. Only surround yourself with the few because, trust me, there are only a few God-ordained people who have been "raised up for your adversity."

If you are angry and upset, particularly wives angry and upset with your husbands; if you cannot play it off, stay home. It is better for you to be at home and protect your witness than to come to church. Everyone will know that you are upset. If you allow them to sense that you are angry with your spouse through your body language, you are starting the rumor mill going. Next thing you know, you will have the "hoochies" who have gotten "the word of the Lord" that your mate should be their spouse and it will be just a matter of time before you have other negative situations that you have to deal with. Does this sound far-fetched? Do you know there are often women waiting in the wings, ready to pounce on any inkling of what may look like trouble in your marriage or trouble in your church?

This same principle applies to your leadership. A public display of dissension among you or your leaders often sends the signals to the Absaloms and the snakes that it is time to come together and attempt a takeover. Even though everything I went through was hard and legitimate, God still held me accountable for my actions. And God will hold you accountable, no matter how much you believe that you have a right to feel like you do. Remember, your issues and problems are not more important than your witness.

There are four things that I advise all of my ministers to do:

1) Stay away from controversial issues.
2) Stay away from controversial people.
3) Stay away from controversial places.
4) Stay away from controversial things.

You may feel like this is bondage, but remember that you must *"give no place to the devil"* (Ephesians 4:27). You must be aware that you are to represent Christ and the ministry. If you do not, the blame will surely fall on you.

CHAPTER SEVEN

PATIENCE

"Let patience have her perfect work that ye may be
perfect and entire, wanting nothing."

James 1:4

Patience is a virtue and a necessary ingredient in being effective in both ministry and life. Without patience, you will blow up, give up, and fail to reach God's plan of destiny for your life, for the lives of your family, and for your ministry. Patience is an often-overlooked component of success in life. Faith alone is not enough. The Bible says, ***"Through faith and patience (you) inherit the promises"*** (Hebrews 6:12). If your great faith is not coupled with great patience, your faith will eventually die out and discouragement will set in. You will become distracted, disappointed, and defeat is certain.

I believe that women are usually more adept at operating in patience than men are. Oftentimes, ladies, you have been sent to help your mates in this area. You have been gifted with the power of persuasion and must use it to help your mate to wait and not jump too quickly to do things.

> *It will be your patience that will see you through your marriage and the ups and downs of ministry.*

For some of you, your patience is necessary for you to successfully deal with issues in your marriage. Your spouse may frustrate you in many areas, and you are justifiably waiting for growth in those areas. You have to remember: All that God spoke concerning your spouse, your marriage, and your family was true. But, you must also remember that ***"better is the end of a thing than the beginning thereof"*** (Ecclesiastes 7:8).

So, it will be your patience that will see you through your marriage and the ups and downs of ministry.

For others, your patience is going to be the key in seeing the development and growth of your children who have been taught, but right now, are not demonstrating the principles and training that you tried to instill in them.

I want to encourage you to *"Let patience have its perfect work"* (James 1:4). Remember that "let" is a term of permission. I have discovered that impatience and pride go hand-in-hand – like kissing cousins. So, it is going to be an act of your will to allow patience to settle in next to your faith. People who struggle with patience must pray to ask God for the grace to remain patient, and quit doing things in their own strength... *"Be strong in the Lord and in the power of <u>His</u> might"* (Ephesians 6:10). Then, after being patient, you just stand still and see the salvation of the Lord.

I believe that the story of Esther is, again, an example of the type of patience that is required to reach your destiny and to follow the plan of God. After being selected as one of the virgins to be presented to King Ahasuerus, the Bible says that the preparation process was one full year. All the time that Esther was inside the palace, she was hiding her ancestry and, certainly, had to have suffered some anxiety and trepidation about having her nationality hidden. She could have succumbed to the pressure, but she waited, had patience, and continued to follow the advice of her uncle Mordecai.

Think about the full implications of this story. Esther had to "hide herself," her traditions, her preferences, her wants and desires for a season – for the sake of a nation. You, too, ladies, often – for a season – must hide yourself, your desires, your wants, and your preferences for the sake of the "nation" or people that you have been called to "save," deliver, and set free.

Continuing in the life of Esther, Haman convinced the king to sign a decree to destroy all of the Jews. One can only imagine the fear and dread that Esther must have felt. However, she could not overreact or respond foolishly (or out of her emotions). She took the time to get sound counsel from her spiritual mentor, Mordecai, and followed all that he advised. Then, in the face of what could have been a very tumultuous situation, she did not just run to the king, even though the Bible was clear that Esther had more favor than any of the women. She waited, fasted, and prayed, and then entered into the presence of the king. This was only after she had taken the time to seek the face of the Lord. She waited until she had counsel. She waited until she had completed her spiritual warfare. God gave her a strategy both naturally and spiritually in that she put on her "royal apparel." In other words, in addition to pulling down spiritual strongholds, the sister made sure she was "fine" when she came into the king's presence. And she looked so good that she caused the king to offer her half of his kingdom!

Do you think she would have gotten the same results if she had heard the news about the decree, panicked, and then rushed into the king's presence? I think not.

Many times, we have very pertinent and serious situations that should cause us to stop and seek God, receive godly counsel if needed, and do the necessary spiritual warfare before we make major decisions or fly off the handle. Too many times, we all have not allowed patience to have its perfect work.

You may have situations right now that, perhaps, should cause panic or depression. Do not allow the enemy to lure you into making a hasty and potentially fatal decision. I am not necessarily talking mortality, but fatality to your marriage, or your business, or your ministry. No matter how serious the issue may be, like Esther, you must be patient, trust God, and watch Him not only bring you out, but bring you out on top! Esther not only saved herself, but the nation was saved and her mentor, Mordecai, ended up being in the second-highest position of power.

Like Esther, God has a perfect plan waiting for your situation, but you will only see it if you allow patience to do its work.

CHAPTER EIGHT

GENEROSITY

"It is more blessed to give than to receive."

Acts 20:35

The ministry is no place for stingy people. A miserly, selfish, and self-centered person will only frustrate the grace of God in ministry. There is unequivocally no place in ministry for such a person. We have to always remember that the moment our ministries and our lives serve our own purposes more than the purposes of God and others, we are no longer servants.

There are four major areas of giving that every woman in ministry must learn, which are:

1. How to share her husband
2. How to share her home
3. How to share her money
4. How to share herself.

SHARING YOUR HUSBAND

If your husband is the pastor, he is the focus of the attention of the church. People do not always follow or understand couth. If you have a problem with people not addressing you or making comments like, "Who is she?" Or, when people speak to him but they do not speak to you, your generous spirit that is full of love and patience must demonstrate grace and dignity. You cannot have a chip on your shoulder or be so insecure that you do not understand that there may be legitimate reasons that people act as they do. Many times, people are just in a hurry and do not mean to overlook you. You cannot take these things personally, but you will need to have an ability to graciously offer your husband's attention to others and the matters of ministry.

If you are an insecure or a jealous woman, you must ask God to help you to overcome your insecurities. There will always be other attractive women and all types of situations that will occur that can potentially make you uncomfortable. You, again, must overcome jealousy in ministry.

It is human nature that people gravitate to the leader. People will come seeking the pastor's wisdom and anointing. Generally, they will love you, but often, they are really not in the ministry for you – although they may love and respect you. Most of your church members were drawn to your church because

> *If you are an insecure or a jealous woman, you must ask God to help you to overcome your insecurities.*

of your husband. Therefore, there is a need to accept the time, responsibility, and commitment that it requires for him to build up the House of God.

I must add that, although the pastor is usually the one to whom members want to talk, I advise all of the pastors under my apostolic covering never to counsel without their wives. It is just foolish in this day and time ever to open any door for the enemy to come in. Support your spouse's commitments as much as possible and be realistic about the time and energy that it takes for him to pour a sure foundation in people, build relationships, and properly communicate to and train leadership.

I have seen too many wives competing for their husbands' attention. They were not willing to make the sacrifice that it takes, particularly in the growing years of the church, when one is properly building a progressive and thriving ministry.

SHARING YOUR HOME

We already know that I Timothy 3:2 tells us that we are to be **"given to hospitality."** The first lady plays a major role in the fulfillment of that Scripture. A true wife will know how to properly care for her husband's guests.

In reality, this has nothing to do with being a first lady; it is just plain good manners. You should greet the guests, making them feel comfortable, fulfilling any need they may have. Never make anyone feel uncomfortable or unwelcome in your home.

Your spouse may bring unexpected guests home with him; or you may have had an argument with your spouse and unexpected guests show up at your door, or unexpected guests show up at your door who are really not unexpected – you soon discover that your spouse forgot to inform you that he invited them. Your response in any of these events must be one of maturity, confirming the fact that you have become that gracious hostess that God has called you to be.

At least 200 of the 365 days in a year, company is in my home. I could not do that unless I had a wife who was generous enough to share our home. I am afraid of first ladies who have never opened up their homes to anyone. Such behavior is indicative of a first lady who has a social problem and may not realize it. I am not suggesting that you open your home to everyone or even to a lot of people, but I believe it is impossible to be very effective in ministry without having some level of intimacy with someone. I am not referring to your congregation. I am referring to other leaders, like pastors, your overseer, or co-laborers with whom God has intended for you to fellowship.

Hospitality was one of the overlooked strengths of the church in the Book of Acts. Didn't the Bible say that they "went from house to house?" Again, in no way am I advocating that pastors or leaders should interact with the sheep on that level or become co-dependent on any person. However, I do know that there is a place, a purpose, and power in such fellowship.

I have often witnessed such gatherings being the opportunity that God uses for his leaders to be encouraged, restored, and delivered. So, you must understand that God uses these types of gatherings for His

> *The Kingdom of God is transferred through relationship.*

purposes. Do not look at them simply from a personal preference.

I believe that the most successful and effective leaders are relational. The Kingdom of God is transferred through relationship. Elijah's anointing was transferred to his spiritual son, Elisha, through relationship. Moses and Joshua; Jesus and His disciples are examples of transference of anointing through relationships, through all of those intimate moments and times of fellowship.

Whether you consider yourself an introvert or extrovert, a sanguine personality or a melancholy, allow the Holy Spirit to guide you and use you and your home to be a place of restoration, reconciliation, recreation, and rejuvenation.

SHARING YOUR MONEY

Look at the woman in Proverbs 31 who we know as the "virtuous woman." This virtuous woman is the prototype of every Christian woman and the giving she displays is a trait that should exist in every child of

> *The first lady ought to be the leader in the church in terms of generosity.*

God – particularly those who are in ministry. Her generosity in giving to others is one of the recurring themes of this awesome woman in Proverbs 31. Verse 15 says that she *"giveth meat to her household and a portion to her maidens."* Verse 20 says she *"stretcheth out her hand to the poor; yea, she reacheth forth her hands to the needy."* It is clear that she takes care of her own house well, but it is just as clear that she also blesses those around her, as well as the needy.

The first lady ought to be the leader in the church in terms of generosity. However, I have to temper what I am saying in order to bring balance. My wife, Denise, was small in stature, yet she was big in giving. She was the most giving person I have ever known.

Unfortunately, usually the biggest suckers for a sad story are those who have the gift of giving. I have not yet seen a person who had a gift of giving who did not have a mercy gift as well. Those two gifts run together, just like the power gifts (the gift of faith and the gift of healing) always go together.

I am not endorsing giving so much that you do it apart from wisdom, because that can cause problems. For instance, I would never give a woman any money unless I talked it over with my wife first – that would not be wise. Yet, there is something wrong in our hearts when we never deny ourselves or our ministry for the sake of others. There is a need now, more than ever, for us, the Body of Christ, to evaluate ourselves in the area of giving.

I had a preacher once tell me that God did not need his money, because God already had all of him. (I think God might be requesting an exchange on that one!) It is appalling to see the number of ministers who are cheap, yet these same ministers exhort the saints to "live by faith."

I believe that how you handle your money is how you handle the anointing. I also believe that money is one of the faith tests that every believer must pass if God is really going to bless you at your greatest potential. Why do I say that? Let's just look in the Bible at the money tests.

Gehazi, who should have inherited Elisha's anointing, which was a double-portion anointing at that, failed the money test. He could not perceive passing up the things that Naaman had offered Elisha and sold out for material blessings. The issue was not that God did not want him to have these things. The issue was as the prophet asked him, *"Is it not the time?"*

God does have the best in store for us, but there is an "appointed time" for that vision to come to pass.

The person we refer to as the rich young ruler in Luke 18 had what most of us would probably consider being an upright, moral, and righteous life. He kept the commandments from his youth; he had gone through the trouble of "seeking" Jesus; but we find out that his seeking would only be on his own terms. When Jesus let the young ruler know what it would really require to seek Him, the Bible says, ***"He went away sorrowful: for he was very rich."*** Jesus let this zealous follower know that there was ***"one thing thou lackest."***

Unfortunately, there are many still today in the Body of Christ who lack the same thing. Yes, you may pray. Yes, you may fast. Yes, you may feed the poor and come to church faithfully. The question is, have you really given God your all? Can you deny yourself that shopping spree or other luxuries and plant seed in another ministry? Have you turned over to Christ and the Kingdom that area where your treasure is? Your treasures lead to the place where your heart dwells.

Many saints, when it comes to giving, do not trust God to provide for their needs. Could this be why statistics state that only 12 percent of the church really tithes?

I want to address tithing, because I believe tithing is very critical, particularly among leaders. I believe that church leaders should give a tithe outside of their ministries to their overseers, spiritual parents, missions, etc...to literally give to God what He requires. When ministers simply tithe to their local church, they are just giving back to themselves. True, it may go for the building project, but it is your building project. I know it does not go directly to you, but indirectly, it still benefits you. Therefore, I believe that we really honor God's tithe when we give outside of ourselves, to other ministries, and trust God to meet our needs.

Many times, it is the woman who is the leader in giving in the home. Apostle Paul took the time to note the key women who supported his ministry and he said, ***"...Not a few prominent Greek women"*** (Acts 17:4) aided in his ministry.

As the woman of both your natural and spiritual house, you must have a healthy, biblical perspective about giving, tithing, and sowing, in order for your house to flourish and continue in the blessings of the Lord. You may even have to help your husband in this area. Utilize the wisdom that God has given you.

Tithing and giving are so critical because through them, God *"rebukes the devourer for your sake"* (Malachi 3:11). I have seen too many leaders struggle in their churches and in their homes for years and years and cry out to God, "What am I doing wrong?" Well, let's start with your tithes and offerings. Are you tithing to your spiritual leader? Thou that teachest others to tithe and honor their leadership, are you doing the same? I cannot tell you how many ministers I have encountered who are in this predicament, yet every dollar they get goes right back to them.

I must clarify that I do understand when you are just starting ministry that you have to put every dime into what you are doing. Have you considered your personal income from your job or from your speaking engagements? You could tithe from those. Some people send their personal tithe to their local church and a church tithe to their overseer, or vice versa. Whatever God leads you to do, you must do it quickly so that you can begin to experience the never-ending supply that comes when you fully obey God and you hold nothing back.

Too many ministers have made their churches their treasure. They are so afraid of "taking money from the church" and laboring over the next project that they have forgotten the principle that brought them that far: *"Give and it shall be given unto you, pressed down and running over..."* (Luke 10:38).

Ladies, you are so critical in this area in your home and ministry that I do not believe I can emphasize it too much. Getting the victory over stinginess, greed, overindulgence, and all the trappings that come along with ministry is often left to the hands of the woman of the house. Abigail understood this principle and saved her own life and the lives of her entire household because, when her husband did not see a need to give, she knew she had to respond to David's request. Abigail's wisdom and generosity saved many lives.

You, too, may have some situations where pride and ego may prevent someone from wanting to give, but that seed sown may be the key to having life and having it more abundantly. It

> *First ladies should be women given to generosity and integrity, having victory over greed.*

44

could be a call to give to an enemy or someone not thought to be worthy, but you must hear God, obey Him, and live.

Lastly, I have counseled many ladies who have attempted to abdicate their responsibilities in this area of financial integrity and tried to place it on their spouses. The story of Ananias and Sapphira let us know that, although the man is the head of the house, the wife will not be found blameless. Why? The Bible says, *"Because she was privy"* (Acts 5:9). If you are privy to any lack of integrity in this area, you will be held accountable if you fail to do anything about it or, worse than that, go along with it. It is no coincidence that the first form of judgment in the New Testament Church involved money. You must be a woman given to generosity and integrity, having victory over greed.

SHARING YOURSELF

One of the key facets of ministry, which follows the example of Jesus Christ, is our daily call "to die" and to deny ourselves. We have to be ever so careful not to get to the place of such comfort, success, and importance that we have stopped dying and stopped denying. When we get to that place, we have become arrogant, prideful, and are no longer servants. We have to die to our own preferences, bad habits, and rude assumptions. We have to die to our own thought life, traditions, and lifestyle, in order to line ourselves up to God's Word and His ways.

There will be times in ministry that God will call you to give yourself to others in such a way that seems unfathomable to others. Ruth had such a charge from God. Ruth was blessed in the end because of her total dedication and commitment to someone (her mother-in-law, Naomi) who had no visible means of being a benefit to her. Naomi was widowed and broke, but Ruth gave of herself to Naomi, because she saw that Naomi held the spiritual impartation that she needed.

You may either be the "Naomi" to give impartations or the "Ruth" to go out of your way to receive one. Either way, it requires you to come out of yourself, out of your comfort zone, and to totally submit your body, soul, and spirit to God and His purposes.

> *After God has your money, your time, and everything you have on the altar, then you are the last thing He requires.*

45

In giving of yourself, there will be times when you will have to ***"comfort the feeble-minded."*** You will have to suppress your flesh and its desires to help, encourage, and even mentor people who you may not have chosen, if God had asked for your opinion. In mentoring them, you will have to hold their hands for a season.

I believe that after God has your money, your time, and everything you have on the altar, you are the last thing He requires. As the leading lady, you must be the first partaker and the prime example of a life that has been totally surrendered to God and His Kingdom's purposes.

I have been appalled at the lack of denial of self I have witnessed among men and women of God. We have begun to operate according to our feelings at an unprecedented level. We know that we are not giving of ourselves when we operate out of our emotions.

I believe one of the best examples of this type of behavior is in the movie, *The Preacher's Wife,* starring Whitney Houston and Denzel Washington. Whitney Houston's character, the first lady, never prayed. She moved by her emotions and got caught up in her own selfish desires and fantasies. As a woman of God, you cannot be a purely emotional being. You will have emotions and emotions demand expression, but you must then submit your emotions to the Word of God and its power, relinquishing any anger, hurt, rebellion, discouragement, envy, jealousy, and desire to the Holy Spirit.

I would like for you to take a few moments right now to ask God to show you any areas in your life that you have not given totally to Him. After He has shown you these areas, please repeat this prayer:

> *Father, in the Name of Jesus, I come before you today, asking that you forgive me of my sin of selfishness. I know that your Word says that if any man desires to follow you, he must deny himself and take up his cross daily. Right now, Father, as I have repented of my lack of denial and selfish ambition, I commit to deny myself of anything that is not pleasing to you. I commit to humble myself to the correction of Your word and Your Holy Spirit, in every area of my life. I will deny myself the right to get even. I will deny myself of overindulgence. I will deny myself of my own opinions and submit all of my ways to you. I will be confident that you will direct, avenge, and establish me in all of my ways. Lord, I take up the cross that you have given me, the burden for*

souls, the purpose for which you have placed me here in this earth, and I leave everything else at your feet. I thank you, right now, Father, that your grace is sufficient, and I can rest in that, because those that fear you have strong confidence. So, I now give you the praise, honor, and glory for the victory! Amen.

CHAPTER NINE

WISDOM

"The fear of the Lord is the beginning of wisdom."

Proverbs 9:10

We know that ***"the fear of the Lord is the beginning of wisdom"***; so, we begin our lifelong wisdom journey when we accept Jesus as our Lord and Savior and reverence Him as the author and finisher of our faith. Therefore, I must begin this chapter on wisdom by emphasizing this very critical point.

"The fear of the Lord" is the reverential respect and awe of God. I believe this is one of the key elements that is missing in our marriages, homes, and ministries. This is why we are not seeing the miracles, signs, and wonders as in the days of old. The fear of the Lord has diminished.

The Bible says that "sound wisdom" is laid up for the righteous. The fear of the Lord, beloved, will stop you from compromising. It will keep you from doing or saying the wrong thing; from being around the wrong people; and from being in the wrong place (at the wrong time). The pure and essential reverence of our Almighty God, who has the power to split every neutron and electron in our bodies, and can put both body and soul into hell, is missing today in the average church and among the average Christian and the average minister.

How can I say these negative things about the church? It is because of many of the abominable, irreprehensible words, thoughts, and activities that exist in the Body of Christ.

Sadly, many of the attitudes, politics, and pervasive ideals are accepted in exchange for celebrity, fame, exposure, and money. There are just some things you would not wear, words you would not say, places you would not go, and actions you would not do if you really have the fear of the Lord. Let us take a look at what the Bible says about the fear of the Lord:

> The fear of the Lord ...
> ...Is the beginning of wisdom (Psalms 111:10)
> ...Is the beginning of knowledge (Proverbs 1:7)

...Prolongeth days (Proverbs 10:27)
...Is strong confidence (Proverbs 14:26)
...Is a fountain of life to depart from the snares of death
    (Proverbs 14:27)
...Is the instruction of wisdom (Proverbs 15:33)
...Tendeth to life: and (he that hath it) shall abide satisfied;
    he shall not be visited with evil (Proverbs 19:22)
...Are riches, honor, and life (Proverbs 22:4)
The churches...walking in the fear of the Lord, and in the comfort
of the Holy Ghost, were multiplied (Acts 9:31).

So, it is an exercise in futility to emphasize wisdom if you do not have a real reverence for God, His Word, His omnipotence, and His power. Why, because reverence is where true wisdom begins.

Many times, it is my fear of the Lord that stops me from saying or doing hurtful things. I know God is loving and forgiving, but I also know that I will reap what I sow. I know God is good and merciful, but the teacher (and leader) will have the greater condemnation. I know God will forgive me and love me always, but I also know that as a man or woman of God in a place of authority, power, and experience, I can disobey Him and end up like Moses – unable to enter my promised land.

Do you have a healthy fear of the Lord that keeps your tongue from evil? Are you always aware that God hears every vow you have made and holds you accountable? Do you fear God enough to know that even if you do not open your mouth, you must daily die to the internal thoughts and activities of your heart that may displease Him? If you do not consciously and actively examine yourself, you do not have the fear of the Lord.

Those who fear the Lord have a hard time judging others, because they know that they are "a wretch undone." Those who fear the Lord do not want to offend Him in any way, not in dress, not in speech, not in actions, nor in associations. Those who fear the Lord inquire of Him and seek His approval and permission in every aspect of their lives. Those who fear God seek godly counsel, knowing that in the multitude of counselors, there is safety. Those who do not fear God make up their own minds and say, "God said it," masking their independent spirit with false spirituality.

I want you to take a few moments to ask God:

1. Have I demonstrated total reliance on You in every area of my life?
2. Have I demonstrated total reverence for You in my marriage, ministry, on my job, as a parent, in relationships, and with my money?

If you need to repent, take the time to do so, and ask the Holy Spirit to teach you how to be "renewed in the spirit of your mind."

Now that you are sure that you have entered on the wisdom route through a healthy fear of the Lord, it is imperative that a "spirit of wisdom" guides you in all that you do.

To have a "spirit of something" means to have the breath, life-giving force, or disposition of something. So, when we operate in the breath and disposition of wisdom, it will bring forth life and health. This principle can be applied to our personal lives, relationships, businesses and ministries.

The marriages and households that have this spirit of wisdom operating in them will be marriages and households that bring life and reflect the image of wisdom in all that is connected to them. Isn't that why Sheba was blown away with Solomon? The Bible says in 1 Kings 10:4-5,

> *"And when the queen of Sheba had seen all Solomon's wisdom, and the house that he had built, and the meat of his table, and the sitting of his servants, and the attendance of his ministers, and their apparel, and his cupbearers, and his ascent by which he went up into the house of the Lord; there was no more spirit in her."*

When she saw his wisdom, how he handled business, how he treated his people, how his servants were dressed, how he decorated the palace, how he was able to answer her questions, the girl fainted!

People should be able to "see" your wisdom, whether it is through how you raise your children, in your marriage, or in your ministry. Unfortunately, in today's "commercialized" society, many who are on television, who have written books and have five-part series on areas of wisdom, if you followed them home, it would be hard to find wisdom.

Make a commitment today that you will make wisdom the principal thing and pray for the "spirit of wisdom" according to Isaiah 11:2. When you begin to operate from the spirit of wisdom and not just simply applying wisdom here and there, your wisdom will be reflected in everything you do. Or, in other words, that spirit will have a "seat" within you, so everything you do will be processed through wisdom.

Where do I start? How do I operate in this spirit? If you have been reading this book with an open spirit, you are already on your way. As you continue to pray, seek the direction of the Holy Spirit, study the word of God, and seek godly counsel, you will begin to make decisions that reflect the disposition of God as opposed to the disposition of your experiences, your opinions, and your preferences. Let me give you an example of the spirit of wisdom in action.

On many occasions, I have had to share some things with wives concerning their husbands (prophetically, pastorally, and psychologically). Please note, I am not referring to violating confidences of spouses or anything of that nature. I am specifically referring to cases requiring me to give both practical and biblical instruction to women who were married to "Nabal."

Now, the wives with a spirit of wisdom took what I shared with them as their spiritual leader, gave it to God, and were led by the Spirit of God what to do and even what to share with their spouses, if anything. The foolish women often repeated everything I shared with them (which was only for their benefit) with "Nabal" — a fool. Now, we know that the Bible says that fools do not receive instruction. So, guess what happened? Most of the time, the fools got offended and angry, and usually the family – and then ultimately the marriage – was destroyed. In contrast, many of the marriages where there was a wise woman in operation were redeemed. Often, the mate later got saved or delivered and their houses were set free.

So, what am I saying? Many times you, as the first lady and the woman of the house, have to be very discerning to the Spirit of the Lord. I believe we would have more unity among the brethren if we had more women of wisdom. You see, even though your friend may have told you that "Bishop Know-it-all" made some disparaging remarks about your husband, if you really hear from God, it may not be wisdom to tell him. The Bible says,

"A fool uttereth his whole mind." You do not need to tell everything you know. Or, if your spouse hears some things that are disturbing to his male ego, you do not chime in and feed his anger, but you speak out of a spirit of wisdom and love, encouraging him and reminding him of what the Word of God says.

Please note that the "spirit of wisdom" is not possibly in operation when the decisions, comments, or actions are in direct opposition to the Word of God. Below are some of what I consider to be some of the "major" areas of wisdom that I believe need to be addressed among God's leading ladies:

Withholding Sex from Their Spouses, for Whatever Reason

Remember, there is no wisdom apart from the Word of God. I wanted to start first with that which is natural. The Bible warns us in 1 Corinthians 7:5 to, *"Defraud ye not one the other, except it be with consent for a time....that Satan tempt ye not for your incontinency."* The same passage also mentions in verse 4 that the woman does not have power over her body, but the husband and vice-versa. So, it is clear that the lack of a sex life will give place to the devil and open the door for adultery, perversion, and other types of sin.

Now, ladies, I need to keep it real right here. Most anointed men have a very strong sexual appetite. Can you say "David"? David was a worshipper and a man after God's own heart. However, you can see by how he went after both Abigail and Bathsheba that he was still just a man, and when he saw a fine woman, he wanted her.

Just check it out in scripture. Judah, Abraham, Sampson – all of them had a time in their lives where they justified their sexual satisfaction in a time of stress.

You do not want to have your husband in such a vulnerable position where he is stressed on his job, stressed at the ministry, and then, because he is not being fulfilled at home, stressed at home. Remember this simple equation:

Stress + Stress + Stress = MIS—STRESS!

I cannot begin to tell you how many saved men of God have either fallen in this area or are struggling with great difficulty, often because of an insensitive wife who has convinced herself that her spouse is too saved to want sex. Please do not make this very unwise mistake.

Preaching/Teaching/Counseling from Your Emotions Rather than from the Spirit of God

Emotions demand expression, but emotions must be managed. We are all emotional beings by nature, but we must *"bring into captivity every thought to the obedience of Christ"* (II Corinthians 10:5) if we are going to be spiritual and walk in wisdom.

I have seen too many women (and, quite frankly, men as well) begin to teach and preach from what they call "revelation," but is actually from the soulish realm where they have been wounded or hurt. For example, you may be going through a divorce, so because you are hurting and upset over your husband's lack of commitment or whatever may have been the problem, you do a ten-week series on "Husbands, Love Your Wives OR ELSE!"

Often, when we have been through traumatic experiences, such as divorce, betrayal, or loss, we really need to check and double-check with God, to make sure that it is not our emotions, our hurt, and our resentment talking, as opposed to the Spirit of God. I have learned not to trust myself in times like that, and stay away from those areas until I know that I can deliver a balanced, Spirit-influenced message, rather than voice my own frustrations under the guise of a sermon. Trust me. I have been there and the result of preaching out of emotions is usually that you will offend, confuse, and possibly even scatter the sheep.

Copying/Mimicking Others Rather than Finding Out Who You Are and Being That Person Perfectly

One of the greatest examples in the Bible of a person knowing who they were and understanding their own strength is David. He was a shepherd boy and he had been trained as such. When David was preparing to fight the giant, Goliath, Saul tried to put his armor on David. David soon realized that he could not fight with anyone else's armor; he had been trained to fight in the sheep field, and he had to trust God that His grace was sufficient.

Have you ever been in the middle of a "fight" and realized you had been trying to fight your battle with somebody else's "armor" and not your own? God has prepared all of us in our own particular "fields," and showed us how to get victory in our battles. Some achieve tremendous results when they fast and pray for twenty-one days. God has trained them and revealed to them that that is their primary weapon of warfare. Am I saying that only some should fast and pray? Of course not. We all should have a lifestyle of fasting and prayer, but there are some saints whom God trains and prepares so that fasting and prayer is their primary weapon of defense.

For others, the weapon of warfare may be in the area of giving. My current wife, Darlyn, shared with me that when she was growing in the Lord, her weapon was often her "seed." As she was going through major traumas and battles, God would challenge her to give a supernatural seed and, as a result, breakthrough would come to her. For Darlyn, giving is her primary weapon.

In whatever way God has prepared you, shown Himself strong in your life, and instructed you, you must be confident in how God has taught you how to fight. Don't try to put on somebody else's weapon because it sounds or looks more spiritual or sensational. Listen to the Spirit of God and be obedient to His instructions for your life.

I am convinced that too many people in ministry are walking around carrying Saul's heavy armor when all they need is a slingshot and five smooth stones. Mimicking others and trying to copy rituals, ministries, mandates, or visions that belong to others will only leave you feeling overburdened and paralyzed.

Failing to Develop Key Relationship Skills
The Kingdom of God is transferred through relationship. Elijah's anointing and mantle was transferred to the person with whom he had the closest relationship. Samuel was mentored and trained through his relationship with Eli. Jesus had to spend three years with the disciples, night and day, in order to transfer the kingdom into their bosom. The disciples would not have been able to continue to advance the kingdom with simply a casual, polite, non-committed relationship with Jesus. They had to spend time with Him, walk with Him, observe Him in His "weakness," and put in the sacrifice that it takes to truly develop relationship.

There is an alarming culture of isolation among ministers and the Body of Christ that hinders us all from benefiting from the skills and abilities of others. The types of relationships that build the kingdom require sacrifice of time and money, being inconvenienced, open to correction and instruction, and denial of fleshly motives and desires. Many times, the first lady is key in bridging these types of relationships between ministers, churches, and families.

Take a look at the Shunnamite woman in 2 Kings 4, starting in verse 8 (emphasis mine):

> *8 And it fell on a day, that Elisha passed to Shunem, where was a great woman; and <u>she constrained</u> him to eat bread. And so it was, that as oft as he passed by, he turned in thither to eat bread.*
>
> *9 And <u>she said</u> unto her husband, Behold now, <u>I perceive</u> that this is a holy man of God, which passeth by us continually.*
>
> *10 Let us make a little chamber, I pray thee, on the wall; and let us set for him there a bed, and a table, and a stool and a candlestick: and it shall be, when he cometh to us, that he shall turn thither.*
>
> *11 And it fell on a day that he came thither, and he turned into the chamber, and lay there.*

This woman is a prime example of the woman of the house having the perception, insight, spirituality, and wisdom to be led by the Spirit of God to connect to right relationships. The Bible says in verse 9 that, ***"She perceived."*** She initiated a relationship with the man of God. There is no indication throughout the entire story of this woman in chapter 4, that her husband ever had much perception, spirituality, or understanding. She continued to be the one who stood in the gap for her child, believed the prophet, and actually was the obvious spiritual leader in her house. It was because of this woman's initiation of relationship with the prophet that she and her husband got their miracle.

Regrettably, there are too many instances where the first lady is actually burning down these types of bridges because of her attitude, selfishness, or lack of understanding of the importance of relationships in ministry, business, and family. First ladies, you are often the key to perceiving right relationships, but you must be able to discern and respond correctly to those whom God has "passing you by continually." I promise you, the right people are in your vicinity. Do you have the relationship skills to properly respond to those to whom God has called for you to reach out?

No matter how successful you and your ministry may be, you have an "infirmity," and God has a relationship established for your infirmity. An infirmity is an area where you are not firm. So, you may have a 30,000-person congregation, but if your marriage is not firm, God has someone with the wisdom to help you and your spouse in your marriage. Or maybe your marriage is fine, but you need wisdom in how to build ministry. Whatever area in which you need help, God has *"a brother born for your adversity"* (Proverbs 17:17). God lets us know that there is someone ordained to assist us in our adverse situations, but we have to be led by the Spirit of God and not so lifted up in pride that we do not want to get help. For God to say he has a brother born for our situation lets us know that the brother (or sister, of course) who has been raised up is the one anointed for that particular challenge in our lives. We often deal with situations too long and go through unnecessary changes because of our lack of relationship-building and our suspicious attitudes, pride and arrogance. "Are not two better than one?"

One of the reasons why many of us struggle with depression, anxiety, addictions, and guilt is that we failed to complete certain developmental tasks when we were growing up. The Bible clearly reveals how strongly God feels about the importance of relationships. God said, *"It is not good that the man should be alone"* (Genesis 2:18). Living in relationships or bonding is the foundation of God's character, which is why God made us – He wanted a relationship with us.

Relationship is our most fundamental need. Without attachment to God and others, we cannot really be ourselves. Failure to bond in the past interferes with bonding in the present. People who never develop an emotional bond to anyone and remain disconnected fear that other people hate them or will hurt them.

People who do not make emotional attachments to God and other people live in a perpetual state of not getting their needs met. We all have three primary needs: to give love, to receive love, and acceptance. Emotional detachment creates a deficit of the primary needs and, as a result, creates isolation.

Isolation is very dangerous and is actually abusive. Ask a prisoner how it feels to be put in isolation. There are many ministers in isolation, some involuntarily, but most often, voluntarily, due to the lack of the development of relationship skills.

Let's examine three stages of isolation:

Stage One: Protest

This is the state of self-pity. The individual feels sad and angry and protests his or her lack of relationships. Poutiness, moodiness, and cantankerousness are common. At this state, the disappointments remain more outward than inward. Common behaviors during this stage include putting up defense mechanisms, such as overworking or concentrating on nothing but business to avoid dealing with the circumstances. During this stage, one begins to deny the need for other people and the desire for relationships.

Stage Two: Depression

At this point, the individual begins to lose hope that his or her needs will ever be met, and depression sets in. Also, the anger and negative meditation about disappointments in past relationships become more inward than outward. Common behaviors during this stage are devaluation and projection. Devaluation occurs when the individual begins to devalue or lessen the importance of love and relationships. Projection occurs during this stage when a person projects or extends his or her personal issues, fears, or values incorrectly to other people.

Stage Three: Detachment

Now the individual is out of touch with both his or her own needs and the needs of others. The individual now operates in a perpetual state of denial, pretending not to need the affirmation and fellowship of others. They fully deny the foundational need for relationships and, ultimately, alter their personality and limit their development and growth.

In its extreme state, this stage can lead to psychotic and deranged behavior. At this stage, the common behavior is called "reaction formation," which means that now the individual does the opposite of what he or she really wants to do. At this state, total denial occurs and is often accompanied by a spirit of self-hatred. Self-hatred develops through both real and perceived rejection.

Now, that we looked at the stages of isolation, you are in a better position to do self-examination.

How are your relationships? Every woman of God needs at least one friend or mentor to whom she can "vent" and with whom she can laugh, receive instruction, or just let down her guard.

If you do not have any friends you need to ask yourself, "Have I shown myself friendly?" (Proverbs 18:24). One translation of this Scripture says,

"If you want friends, be a friend." Do you often talk yourself out of forming relationships? Are you easily offended or lack trust when it comes to forming bonds with people? You may not believe this is spiritual, but your ability to relate to people is very spiritual. As a matter of fact, God has a problem with people who pretend to be so spiritual and close to Him, yet cannot even get along with other people. 1 John 4:20 puts it this way, ***"If a man say, I love God and hateth his brother, he is a liar: for he that loveth not his brother whom he hath seen, how can he love a God whom he hath not seen?"***

No matter what you have been through, you have to trust somebody. You will miss out on some of the most fulfilling and profitable relationships if you shut off yourself, your family, or ministry from godly, productive relationships because of fear, distrust, and suspicions.

I am by no means saying that you should reveal intimate details to a lot of people. There are some things you only share with your spouse. However, I am saying that you need healthy, godly intimacy with people of like minds and hearts. If you have been hurt and wounded, I want to encourage you to move beyond the betrayal, disloyalty, and hurt to find that sister (or brother) who has been raised up to bring healing, encouragement, and help to your life.

Please remember that if you are struggling in this area, you have a root of unforgiveness that must be broken. There is nothing that has happened to you that you are not required to forgive. I know that it's tight – but it's right!

I, personally, know the power of relationships and how God will use them to restore your soul. I have been wounded in relationships through betrayal, disloyalty, slander, lies, abuse, etc. ...so I understand how hard it is to trust anybody when you go through a season where it looks like you have been hurt by everybody! However, I am a witness that God will "restore the years that the cankerworm and the palmerworm have eaten...." If a mate has wounded you, God can restore that. If church people have wounded you, God will heal your wounds. Maybe you were abused as a child by authority figures; God will bring you spiritual authority figures who will correctly teach you submission through love.

I have noticed that most of the time, when God restores you, He gives you back more than what you thought you lost. All of the relationships that wounded me, God replaced those relationships with people who far exceeded the standards, talents, abilities, and commitment levels of the people over whom I had previously grieved. Trust God today to lead you to right relationships.

Remaining a Lady
It is very important for all of the leading ladies to remember the responsibility that comes along with leadership. Strong, powerful, and anointed women of God can still be ladies, still lead, take care of business, pastor churches, walk in apostolic authority or whatever God has ordained you to do, and remain a lady.

There are many women today who do not seem to realize that even though you are in a leadership role, you still need a level of wisdom as you lead both men and women, if you want them to follow you. Yes, I know that it can be difficult for strong women, because some men do not want to be led by women. Nonetheless, with your power of persuasion and the spirit of wisdom in operation, you will be able to accomplish all that has been assigned to you without being difficult, moody, cantankerous, and generally not spoken of in a positive manner because of your attitude.

Women in particular must have the Spirit of God as they take on the roles in the kingdom that God has for them. I personally know that God is using women in this season in a very special way, but I also know that they are going to need to know how to remain "ladies" just as much as they know how to preach, prophesy, cast out devils, and lead a nation. Remember, you have the power of persuasion like no other; and if you develop the patience, power, and perseverance that it takes to persuade, you will save nations like Esther, win wars like Jael, and proclaim victories like Deborah!

CHAPTER TEN

WALKING IN YOUR DESTINY

Now that I have spoken to you as a father and overseer (both of which I am), my prayer is that you would be like the Bereans, who received the word of Apostle Paul with all readiness of mind and searched the Scriptures daily, whether those things were so (Acts 17:10-11). Study the Scriptures pertaining to godly living as saints of God and, more specifically, as godly women. Allow the Holy Spirit to minister the truth of His Word and bring conviction for change.

God has placed gifts and talents in you and planned destiny for you before the foundations of the world. My desire for you is that you walk out your manifested destiny as the powerfully anointed woman of God that He has made you; and that your life will be like that of the virtuous woman of God in Proverbs 31, where your children (naturally and/or spiritually) will rise up and call you blessed; and your husband – not only will he call you blessed, but he will continue to praise you (Proverbs 31:28).

Finally, God gave us examples of godly women in His Word, so that the leading ladies in ministry who come after them would learn from them. So, take your place among the Ruths, the Esthers, and the other virtuous first ladies and women of God and watch God use you to turn the world upside down!

ABOUT THE AUTHOR

Clifford E. Turner, Ph.D., one of America's leading Apostles, shares his knowledge and scriptural wisdom on how women in ministry, particularly First Ladies, must exhibit character and behavior commensurate to their call. Apostle Turner utilizes thirty years of experience in ministry to communicate the common attributes of women of God who not just obtain, but maintain their power, influence and authority to transform nations and generations. Having released thousands of women in ministry and being mentored by a female Apostle, Dr. Turner has a special revelation and appreciation of the anointing, grace, and power that God has entrusted to women. In "The Ministry (& Myth) of the First Lady", Apostle Turner clearly separates the smart woman from the wise woman.

Apostle Clifford E Turner, Ph. D. is also an Emmy award-winning writer, producer, and director. For information about his television and film products visit:
www.holywoodstudios.org or www.awakening.com

To obtain more information about Liberty International Network and Apostle Clifford E. Turner visit:
www.libertytemple.org

Other books by Apostle Clifford E. Turner, Ph. D.:
Recovery
"Understanding and Dealing with Life's Traumas"
To order, visit: **www.cedarlifepublishing.com** or call toll free
866-467-4337

To Contact Author, write:
Clifford E. Turner Ministries
P.O. Box 2759
Spring Valley, CA 91979-2759
Phone – (866)-900-CETM (2386)
Email – cetministries@aol.com

Printed in the United States
49270LVS00007B

9 781425 925864